Beauty and the BEAST

A Page to Panto script
by
Joe Meloy

Beercott

Beauty and the Beast
A pantomime in 2 acts

First Published in Great Britain in 2023 by Beercott Books.

Copyright: © Joe Meloy 2023

ISBN:978-1-7393020-2-3

Joe Meloy has asserted his rights to be identified
as the author of this book.

Title is fully protected under copyright. All rights, including professional and
amateur stage production, recitation, lecturing, public reading, motion picture,
radio broadcasting, television and the rights of translation into foreign
languages are strictly reserved.

A catalogue record of this book is available from the British Library.

No one shall make any changes to the play for the purpose of production. No
part of this book may be reproduced, stored in a retrieval system, or
transmitted in any form, by any means, now known or yet to be invented. This
includes mechanical, electronic, photocopying, recording, videotaping, or
otherwise, without the prior written permission of the publisher. No one shall
upload this title, or part of this title, to social media websites.

Professional and amateur producers are hereby warned that title is subject to a
licencing fee. Publication of this play does not imply availability for
performance. Both amateurs and professionals considering a production are
strongly advised to apply to the agent before starting rehearsals, advertising,
or booking a theatre. A licence fee must be paid whether the title is presented
for charity or gain and whether or not admission is charged.

Worldwide licence enquiries for this title should be directed to:
licencing@beercottbooks.co.uk.
Title subject to availability.

www.beercottbooks.co.uk

Beercott

For Jai Groves,

love you mate.

CHARACTERS

BELLE - An intelligent girl who likes to read, always like to think the best of everyone.

MAURICE - Belle's Father, a kind man who loves his daughter more than life itself.

FAIRY DUST - A magical Fairy who helps guide the story, as well as help out when she's needed.

BEAST/PRINCE BEAUMONT - A Prince cursed by a Witch to live as a Beast, hoping to break the spell.

LUCAS LUXURIANT - An arrogant man, set on marrying Belle with or without her or her Father's blessing

BEAUREGARD BURKE - One of Lucas's almost useless henchmen, though he is only there as he's really too scared to say anything to Lucas

MARCEL MARSEILLE - Another of Lucas's almost useless henchmen, just like Beauregard he is only there out of fear of Lucas as well

POTTY PIERRE (COMIC) - The son of Madame Marie Macaroon, he works as the pot wash at the Castle for the Beast

MADAME MARIE MACAROON (DAME) - A kind-hearted woman who used to look after the Beast when he was a baby, also the cook at the Beast's castle

THE WOLF

MALE VILLAGER 1

MALE VILLAGER 2

FEMALE VILLAGER 1

FEMALE VILLAGER 2

CHILD VILLAGER 1

VILLAGERS (ENSEMBLE)

SCENES

SET IN 18TH CENTURY FRANCE

ACT 1

SCENE 1 - In front of tabs / Village Square

SCENE 2 - The Beast's Castle

SCENE 3 - The Outskirts of the Village

SCENE 4 - The Beast's Castle

SCENE 5 - The Outskirts of the Village

SCENE 6 - The Beasts Castle

ACT 2

SCENE 1 - The Village Square

SCENE 2 - The Beast's Castle

SCENE 3 - The Forest

SCENE 4 - The Outskirts of the Village

SCENE 5 - The Beast's Castle

SCENE 6 - In front of tabs / The Castle

SCENE 7 - Bows.

ACT ONE

SCENE ONE

IN FRONT OF TABS/THE VILLAGE SQUARE

FAIRY: Bonjour to one and all,
I'm Fairy Dust, in me of course you can trust!
Welcome to our tale
Our story will unfold, with heroes' brave and bold!
We begin in the depths of France,
Where a Beast is cursed and awaits the spells' reverse
Our Beast was once a handsome Prince,
But he was arrogant and mean, a real sight to be seen
Only love could break the curse
But who in the least could love a beast?
An enchanted rose held the Prince's fate
When the last petal was to drop, the curse could never stop
A Beast forever seems unfair!
Let's start our story, to the French Village of *(local reference)* in all its glory!

(Curtains open to reveal the French Village of (local reference) in full swing)

Song 1 – BELLE & CHORUS

(Song Ends and BELLE takes centre stage)

BELLE: Oh, hello there everyone and welcome to our wonderful little village of *(local reference)*! My name's Belle and I live here in this lovely little French village with my father. Life here is so wonderful, we've got the Pier with all of its fantastic rides and sweet treats, we've got a lovely prom to walk along, which is so wonderful when the sun is shining like it is today! And best of all, I've just read the most amazing book!

VILLAGER 1: What book was it this time Belle?

VILLAGER 2: Yes, please tell us!

BELLE: *(Change this description to suit the Panto performed last year)* It was a tale about a street rat who turned into a Prince! And it had a genie, a flying carpet, a Princess, and of course it all ended happily ever after

CHILD VILLAGER 1: Aladdin? *(Or name of Panto performed last year)*!

BELLE: Yes, that's the one!

CHILD VILLAGER 1: Aladdin *(Or name of Panto performed last year)*, that's so last year

BELLE: Well I still enjoyed it. I can't wait to read another fantastic story! Books are so fantastic, I love to read! And I love living here with all of you

MAURICE: *(From offstage)* Belle! Belle!

BELLE: That'll be Father, I'm just over here Father!

(Enter MAURICE)

MAURICE: Ah! Belle, there you are *(BELLE and MAURICE hug)*

BELLE: Did you have a good trip Father?

MAURICE: I did indeed, I saw so many wonderful things! But the most wonderful thing is coming back home to you *(he presents BELLE with a rose)*. A rose for my beautiful daughter, Belle!

BELLE: Father you needn't bring me a rose from every one of your trips!

MAURICE: Belle, I will forever bring you a rose back from every trip. I don't have much, but I can always bring you back a rose from my adventures!

BELLE: Oh Father thank you so much, it's beautiful.

MAURICE: Anything for you my dear! Though, I do have to tell you some rather unfortunate news. I heard that Lucas Luxuriant will be visiting once again…

FEMALE VILLAGER 1: *(Excited)* Did you say Lucas Luxuriant is coming?

MAURICE: Yes, he is indeed-

FEMALE VILLAGERS: *(All scream with excitement whilst Female VILLAGER 1 begins to swoon)*

BELLE: I just don't understand why you all think he's so handsome! He might look alright on the outside, but inside he's mean and a bully!

FEMALE VILLAGER 2: I can see him coming!

MALE VILLAGER 1: I can see him *(screams like an over excited school girl and fans himself)*

*(We hear LUCAS LUXURIANT with his sidekick
BEAUREGARD BURKE approaching)*

BEAUREGARD: Ladies and Gentlemen, please be upstanding.

MARCEL: Clap and cheer and go crazy with excitement for the most glamourous and handsome man you'll ever be fortunate enough to lay your eyes upon!

BEAUREGARD: The one and only, Lucas Luxuriant!

Song 2 – LUCAS – Filthy Gorgeous by Scissor Sisters (edited lyrics)

LUCAS: When you're strollin' down the street And the ladies start to shout who is this And the ladies that I meet
Run around and scream that you can't miss this
Cos I'm huggin' and I'm kissin' cos they never let me go
All the girls are gonna swarm when muscles they're on show
I'm a pretty, fittie, little cheeky, modest kind of perfect person
'Cause I'm handsome Oooh, and I'm gorgeous 'Cause I'm handsome Oooh, and I'm gorgeous
I'm delicious
Oooh, and I'm lovely And you can't have me
Oooh 'cause I'm not yours

(Spoken)

Bonjour peasants, I have come to grace you with my presence. I'm so gorgeous sometimes, I think it's unfair!

(Singing)

When I'm runnin' from a woman
Cos she's ugly, and she makes me hurl I'm a modest kind of man
But, I wouldn't date ugly girl
You gotta keep yourself together Or you'll faint and hit the ground I'm not even gonna listen
So just turn yourself around
I'm a hunky, funky, little flirty, modest kind of perfect person
'Cause I'm handsome Oooh, and I'm gorgeous 'Cause I'm handsome Oooh, and I'm gorgeous
I'm delicious
Oooh, and I'm lovely And you can't have me
Oooh 'cause I'm not yours
'Cause I'm handsome Oooh, and I'm gorgeous
'Cause I'm handsome Oooh, and I'm gorgeous

I'm delicious
Oooh, and I'm lovely And you can't have me
Oooh 'cause I'm not yours
'Cause I'm handsome Oooh, and I'm gorgeous 'Cause I'm
handsome Oooh, and I'm gorgeous
I'm delicious
Oooh, and I'm lovely And you can't have me
Oooh 'cause I'm not yours

LUCAS: *(He is incredibly French)* Ello, all you beautiful people. If you don't know who I am zen I pity you, for everyone all across ze land knows ze name Lucas Luxuriant. Zer is no man more handsome *(strikes a pose smiling at a group of women who scream an jump with glee)*, zer is no man more intelligent *(he strikes another pose)* and zer is absolutely no man stronger than me *(BEAUREGARD hands LUCAS a phone book, which LUCAS rips in half with ease)*. Hang on *(spotting the audience)* it looks as though we av' some new people ere'. If all of ze ugly people could move down to ze front… Oh, you av' *(He laughs)*. Allow me to properly introduce myself to you all, my name is Lucas and I am ze best at everything. Name something and I bet I am the best;

BEAUREGARD: Chess?

LUCAS: I am ze best

MARCEL: Football?

LUCAS: Ze best, of course!

BEAUREGARD: Dancing?

LUCAS: *(The intro to Blinding Lights by The Weekend starts playing and LUCAS (shadowed by BEAUREGARD and MARCEL) performs the famous short dance routine that went viral via TikTok)* Need I say more?

MARCEL: Certainly not Sir, you are the best!

LUCAS: Ze best! Don't you just love me? *(Audience: No!)* Oh, shut up you peasants! I wouldn't ask any of you your opinion, you're all far too ugly… Oh and whatever you do, don't you dare ever, and I mean ever, boo me, I do not like it. *(Audience: boo!)* Stop it, I said stop it! When my hand goes up, you go silent *(Audience: Boo)*. Beauregard, it doesn't seem to be working.

BEAUREGARD: No Sir.

LUCAS: Whatever, I do not care!

BELLE: Oh yes you do!

LUCAS: Oh no I don't!

BELLE: Oh yes you do!

LUCAS: Oh no I don't!

BELLE: Oh yes you do!

LUCAS: Oh, stop it! *(Realising it's BELLE)* Ah Belle, my beauty. Everyone be gone I need a moment alone with my future wife!

(BEAUREGARD and MARCEL hurry everyone off stage. Exit CHORUS. BEAUREGARD and MARCEL remain on stage.)

BELLE: *(To MAURICE)* Don't worry Father, I'll be fine, I'll see you at home

MAURICE: Very well Belle, I'll see you at home *(Exit MAURICE)*

LUCAS: Beauregard, Marcel?

BEAUREGARD & MARCEL: Yes Sir?

LUCAS: When I said everyone, I meant everyone.

BEAUREGARD: Why yes of course Sir. *(BEAUREGARD does not leave)*

LUCAS: Beauregard?

BEAUREGARD: Yes Sir?

LUCAS: You are everyone.

BEAUREGARD: No, Sir, I am Beauregard.

MARCEL: And I am Marcel

LUCAS: Marcel?

MARCEL: Yes Sir?

LUCAS: Go a-way.

MARCEL: What just me?

LUCAS: Both of you

BEAUREGARD: Which way would you like us to go Sir?

LUCAS: I don't care, just leave.

BEAUREGARD: Very good Sir, we will leave. *(Sad music begins to accompany BEAUREGARD'S speech)* All alone we will leave…

MARCEL: …We'll just be going *(hopefully the audience will start to aww, if they don't MARCEL should gesture that they should)*, that's it we're going…

LUCAS: *(to the audience)* Do not aww them! Now both of you be gone!

BEAUREGARD: *(Sad music still playing)* Oh I'm so upset, I'm bereft, alone and all by myself!

LUCAS: *(To BEAUREGARD)* What are you doing?

MARCEL: Acting, maybe you should try it sometime!

LUCAS: Get off! *(BEAUREGARD & MARCEL both exit quickly).* *(Turning his attention to BELLE)* Now Belle, my gorgeous little thing!

BELLE: I am not your gorgeous little thing!

LUCAS: Why fight what we av'?

BELLE: We do not have anything!

LUCAS: Any women in zis land would throw themselves at me, why do you resist my magnificent physique?

BELLE: Because I see what you are on the inside and that's ugly! You're mean and rude, and I would certainly never want to marry a man as vile as you!

LUCAS: But what is on the inside is nothing, when you get to look at zis all day every day!

BELLE: May I go now please?

LUCAS: Very well, but rest assured one day you will be my wife!

BELLE: I wouldn't marry you if you were the last human on earth! Goodbye! *(Exit BELLE)*

LUCAS: Goodbye Belle. *(To the audience)* I know what you're all thinking, she's crazy for not wanting *(gesturing to himself)* zis. Aren't I just the most stunning man you've ever seen? *(Audience: No!)* Oh shut up, one day Belle will marry me! And zer is nothing you can do about it *(evil laugh)*

(Blackout)

SCENE TWO

THE BEAST'S CASTLE

FAIRY: So, we've been to the village
        But what of the Beast? For this we travel a few miles east
        We arrive at the Beast's castle
        The Kingdom of *(local reference)*, glancing through the haze
        Let us go behind the castle walls
        And meet the Prince, who has been cursed a beast ever since

(Exit FAIRY)

Song 3 – THE BEAST

BEAST: *(Holding the enchanted rose)*. As the petals fall my fate
        becomes more and more bleak, when the last petal falls, I'll be
        stuck as this hideous beast forever. Why couldn't I have been
        nice? I was far too concerned with how I looked rather than
        how others felt! And now I'm destined to live life ugly and
        alone. Curse that witch who cast this spell on me! *(The BEAST
        lets out a massive roar)*.

        *(Blackout. The lights comeback up and the BEAST has
        disappeared, though the Enchanted Rose remains placed at the
        side of the stage)*

(Enter POTTY PIERRE)

PIERRE: *(He runs on with great pace)* I can't stop I've got to sort out
        the Master's dinner *(Stops mid-sentence and sees the audience
        properly for the first time)* Oh, hang on I don't think we've got
        enough food for all of you! We only just have enough for the
        Prince, well, more beast than Prince these days! Have you seen
        him yet? I promise you he's not all bad! Hang on a minute, I
        haven't introduced myself! My name is Pierre, though people
        around here call me Potty Pierre because I'm the pot wash in
        the kitchen, well actually I'm also the second cook, cleaner,
        flower arranger, butler and everything else! You see there use to
        be a whole load of staff who worked here serving the Prince,
        before he had his accident… Well before he was cursed by a
        witch to live as a Beast. All the rest of the staff got too scared of
        him when he became a beast, but me and my Mum stayed, my
        Mum was the Prince's Nanny when he was a baby you see, and
        she couldn't bear the thought of leaving him here all by himself,
        so we stayed. But ever since the Prince turned into a Beast,
        there's been no royal balls or big dances, so me and Mum

haven't been paid a wage in years, we're so poor! *(audience: aww)* Oh we're poorer than that *(audience: aww)* we're even poorer than that! *(audience: aww)*

In fact, we're so poor we have to get our chocolate raisins from the rabbit hutch! No honestly, they're quite good, here! *(throws some out to the audience)* We're so poor at KFC we had to lick other people's fingers! The jokes aren't going to get any better trust me! We're so poor that we couldn't afford to have a family dog, we use to have to take it in turns to go outside and bark. You know what we're so poor that we sometimes can't afford to eat, for dinner Mum would just read the recipes out, and I'm hard of hearing, so I almost starved to death! Here hang on a minute, I know what'll cheer me up! Do you fancy being my friends? *(Ad lib as needed)* great well when I come onstage, I'm going to come on and say, Hiya Gang! And you shout back 'Hiya Pierre!' Shall we give it a go? *(Ad lib as needed)* Right I'm going off! Ready? *(goes off)* Hiya Gang! *(Audience: Hiya Pierre!)* Did you say anything? You did? Well let's try it again then! *(goes off)* Hiya Gang! *(Audience: Hiya Pierre!)* Oh great that's more like it! I'm so glad we're all friends!

(The intro to song four begins)

That'll be my Mum I best get going she'll go mad if she sees me here, I've still got so many pots to wash! Bye for now gang!

Song 4 – MARIE

(Song Ends MADAME MARIE MACAROON takes centre stage)

MARIE: Oh, Hello boys and girls! I'm sure we can do better than that! Hello Everyone! That's much better. What a lovely looking lot we've got in tonight! Honestly, you're the best audience we've had in tonight! Do you like my frock boys and girls? It's my special American dress, one yank and it's off! Well, how silly of me boys and girls I haven't introduced myself, my name is Madame Marie Macaroon, but you can all call me Marie and you *(pointing to a man on the front row)* can call me anytime you like! I work here at the castle with my son Pierre, we're servants to the Beast. Have you seen him yet? *(audience: yes!)* Oh, you have, I promise you underneath all that fur is a charming, caring Prince who's not that scary at all! Oh, how I wish that a beautiful girl would come along and break the spell. All the beast has to do is find someone to fall in love with and the curse will be broken! But it has a time limit, look over there, *(pointing towards the enchanted rose)* when the last petal falls the Prince will remain a beast forever! In fact, that Enchanted Rose is so important that I need to make sure nobody takes it. Actually, boys and girls will you help me out? Well will you? Well if you see anyone going to grab that Enchanted Rose will you shout for me as loud as you can? I'll tell you what, we'll have a practice. I'm going to sneak up to it pretending to be someone else and can you all shout 'Marie!' as loud as you can? Okay good let's give it a go *(MARIE goes to sneak up to the Enchanted Rose)*. Well, did you shout for me? Well I never heard you! Let's try it again *(MARIE sneaks up to the Enchanted Rose again)* I'll tell you what, once more for luck! *(MARIE sneaks up to the Enchanted Rose again. This time the audience are so loud it nearly knocks MARIE off her feet)* Oh! That was much better!

(Enter PIERRE)

PIERRE: Hiya Gang! *(audience: Hiya Pierre!)*. Oh hi Mum!

MARIE: Pierre, have you washed all those pots?

PIERRE: I have indeed Mum!

MARIE: Good because we've got to make the Beast's dinner!

PIERRE: Very well, I'll go and fire up the cooker!

MARIE: No need Pierre!

PIERRE: Why's that Mum?

MARIE: Well I have this brand-new dinner machine!

PIERRE: Wow a new dinner making machine! How does it work Mum?

MARIE: Well it's actually very simple

PIERRE: Really? Are you sure it won't go wrong and make a mess?

MARIE: No, it shouldn't make any mess, because this dinner machine is flawless!

PIERRE: No, we've still got a floor Mum

MARIE: What?

PIERRE: You said it's floorless

MARIE: Yes, and if I call you brainless, I'd be right

PIERRE: What?

MARIE: Look be quiet and listen to me! All you have to do is stand over here *(facing the left-hand side of the stage)* And you say whatever you want for dinner. Ready watch me; Dinner machine could I have some ice cream please *(a hand pops out from the wing with a bowl of ice cream)* See it's easy!

PIERRE: Can I try?

MARIE: Yes, go on son, however let me just get rid of this bowl

PIERRE: How are you going to do that?

MARIE: Easy, heads! *(throws the bowl offstage right)*

PIERRE: *(Stands stage left)* Okay, can I have a pot noodle please? *(A stage hand appears with an unopened pot noodle, PIERRE takes the pot noodle only to realise it isn't cooked)* Can I have some water with it please? *(A stream of water from stage left hits PIERRE directly in the face)*

MARIE: Clean up! *(The entire chorus appears from all different sides of the stage and instantly dries any water that has been left onstage as well as over acting cleaning anywhere else)*

PIERRE: Where did they all come from?

MARIE: They came free with the machine

PIERRE: Oh right, seems like a bargain! Clean up!

(The chorus come on and clean PIERRE, the first chorus member rubs soap all over his face from a big bucket with soap written on it, the soap is shaving foam or some form of slosh. The second member of the chorus comes on with a super soaker water gun on which is written 'water' and sprays PIERRE in the face cleaning off the soap, then several more members of the chorus dry him with a towel and spray his armpits with deodorant)

MARIE: *(After the chorus has cleaned PIERRE)* Much better! Now when you go to the machine next time you need to be more specific!

PIERRE: Okay, right *(goes stage left)* Can I please have a McDonalds, no wait a KFC, no wait Pizza Hut-

(The entire chorus comes on from all different areas sings two lines of the fast food song with the actions)

CHORUS: A pizza hut, a pizza hut, Kentucky fried chicken and a pizza hut! McDonalds, McDonalds, Kentucky fried chicken and a pizza hut!

(Chorus exits quickly and manically)

PIERRE: That didn't even make sense! It didn't even give me any food! And I'm still hungry!

MARIE: Look watch me *(Goes stage left)* Can I please have a cheeseburger *(A cheeseburger is handed onstage by a stagehand)*

PIERRE: What?! How comes it doesn't work for me? *(Goes stage left)* Can I please have- *(PIERRE gets sprayed with water before he even finishes his sentence)*

MARIE: *(Shouting offstage left as if shouting at the stagehand)* Bit trigger happy there weren't you, the poor boy hadn't even finished his sentence! Right try again son!

PIERRE: *(Goes stage left)* Can I just have a glass of water! *(This time the water is sprayed stage right at the unsuspecting MARIE, who goes to walk stage right but slips in the water)* Clean up!

(The chorus once again comes onstage and dries the water onstage and gets MARIE back to her feet again)

MARIE: They're efficient!

PIERRE: I know, what a cast!

MARIE: I think this machines on the blink

PIERRE: Hang on I'll give it one more go *(Goes stage left)* Can I please have a big cream pie? *(the stagehand delivers a cream pie directly into PIERRE'S face. MARIE laughs, as she is laughing she walks over to stage right and gets a pie from a stage hand directly in her face)*

(The BEAST Enters)

BEAST: What on earth is going on?!

PIERRE: Mum got this new machine-

BEAST: It looks as though the whole place needs a good clean up!

MARIE & PIERRE: No!

(The chorus enter manically from all sides of the stage cleaning

everywhere, two of the chorus have water guns which they clean (spray) the audience with. The BEAST stands confused at the back during the ongoing chaos and PIERRE and MARIE are given a towel each to clean their faces off or any mess that maybe on their costumes as the chorus clean everywhere frantically ensuring they actually make sure the floor is dry and there are no slip hazards left afterwards.)

BEAST: *(Let's out a huge roar)* Everybody get out!

(The chorus exit as they entered manically and from all different areas of the stage and auditorium PIERRE and MARIE leave as well, leaving the beast alone onstage)

BEAST: What about my dinner?

(Blackout)

SCENE THREE

THE OUTSKIRTS OF THE VILLAGE

BELLE: Father, must you go away again?

MAURICE: If you enjoy eating, then I must go to work.

BELLE: Well don't be too long! And will you bring me back a rose again?

MAURICE: *(Said with a smile)* Don't I always?

BELLE: I'll see you soon Father!

> *(MAURICE exits off. Enter LUCAS followed by BEAUREGARD & MARCEL)*

LUCAS: Ah Belle, my beauty, my future wife-

BELLE: Oh no not you again! Can't you just leave me alone?

LUCAS: Not until you tell me why you won't be my wife

BELLE: You have an awful personality, you're mean, self-centred, arrogant, egotistical and an over-egged pretty boy!

LUCAS: So, you think I'm pretty?

BELLE: Yes! Pretty ugly!

LUCAS: Ugly?! *(Begins to fall about as if he is going to faint)* Oh Beauregard catch me!

> *(BEAUREGARD puts out his arms to catch LUCAS, but LUCAS falls the other way, also knocking over MARCEL. LUCAS gets up and dusts himself off as does MARCEL)*

LUCAS: I'm not ugly!

BELLE: Oh yes you are!

LUCAS: Oh no I'm not!

BELLE: Oh yes you are!

LUCAS: Oh no I'm not!

BELLE: Oh yes you are!

LUCAS: Oh, shut up! I am ze most beautiful man who has ever lived and one day you will realise that and fall madly in love with me. *(Grabs BELLE by the arm tightly and pulls her in)* Now you listen to me, you'll be my wife whether you like it or not!

BELLE: No, I won't! *(BELLE stamps LUCAS'S foot, he jumps about holding his foot. BELLE goes to run off, BEAUREGARD and MARCEL stand in her way and BELLE confronts BEAUREGARD and MARCEL without even touching them and they both run off scared. Exit BELLE)*

LUCAS: She has gone! Well mark my words, one day that girl will be mine even if I have to force her to marry me, and there's not a thing you lot can do about it! *(Evil laugh)* Beauregard!

(BEAUREGARD & MARCEL run back on)

BEAUREGARD: Yes, Sir?

LUCAS: I will marry Belle one day!

MARCEL: Well-

LUCAS: What do you mean well?!

BEAUREGARD: I mean that maybe you should get married for love-

LUCAS: What has love got to do with getting married!?

MARCEL: Well-

LUCAS: I think you two need to remember who ze boss is!

Song 5 – LUCAS, BEAUREGARD & MARCEL

(Blackout)

SCENE FOUR

THE BEAST'S CASTLE

(Enter MAURICE who is tired and lost)

MAURICE: Hello, is anyone here? I'm terribly sorry to interrupt. I've foolishly got myself a little bit lost on the road- hang on what's that rose over there doing *(MAURICE goes toward the rose, hopefully the audience shout 'Marie!')*

MARIE: Oi! Hands off my rose! *(She clocks eyes with MAURICE)* Oh well hello there you gorgeous hunk of man, what brings you to these parts?

MAURICE: Well I was on my way to deliver a present for work and I got a bit lost

BEAST: *(From offstage)* Who dares to enter my castle!

MAURICE: Who is that?

MARIE: That's our Master! Runaway now!

MAURICE: Runaway? I'm sure I can talk to him.

MARIE: I doubt that-

(the BEAST enters terrifying MAURICE)

BEAST: *(To MAURICE)* You! How dare you enter my home!

MAURICE: I only came in because-

BEAST: *(Notices his Enchanted Rose)* You came to take the rose!

MAURICE: No, though I do always collect a rose for my daughter-

BEAST: And you thought you'd take this one!

MAURICE: No, I-

BEAST: Silence!

MARIE: Sir, if I could just but in-

BEAST: No, you may not!

MARIE: If you could just calm down-

BEAST: I AM CALM! Now you! *(to MAURICE)* listen to me, you may have a rose. Pierre! Pierre! Bring me a rose!

PIERRE: *(Enters in a rush with a rose)* Hiya Gang! Good job I was in the middle of gardening! What do you want a rose for Sir?

BEAST: *(To MAURICE)* What is your name?

PIERRE: It's Pierre, you know that you just called me-

BEAST: Silence!

MAURICE: My name is Maurice

BEAST: Maurice, you may take this rose *(BEAST hands the rose to MAURICE)*, but in exchange the very first person you see, you must send them here to live with me forever! And if you don't adhere to what I have told you, I will find you and drag you back here to live in the dungeon forever more!

MAURICE: *(Scrambles out of the door and exits off quickly)* Thank you Sir

(Blackout)

SCENE FIVE

THE OUTSKIRTS OF THE VILLAGE

(Enter MAURICE as if he's ran all the way from the castle)

MAURICE: My goodness I need to have lay down. I'm feeling rather out of breath. *(Sits down against a rock)*

(Enter BELLE)

BELLE: Father, Father!

MAURICE: No Belle, why did it have to be you, I could have seen anyone else first, but why you!

BELLE: Oh Father, you sound delirious, are you alright?

MAURICE: I was until I saw you-

BELLE: But, I thought you'd be pleased to see me!

MAURICE: On any other occasion I would be.

BELLE: Then what's so different about this one?

MAURICE: I don't even know where to begin!

BELLE: The start is always the best place to begin, that's how I start with any book I read.

MAURICE: Well, I was off travelling for work as you know and I got a bit lost and off the beaten track and I ended up in a strange castle to shelter from the cold outside and inside the castle, I met a lovely woman there, but that didn't last long, as soon a beast appeared-

BELLE: A beast?

MAURICE: Yes, a walking talking beast and he spared me my life, on the condition that the first person I laid eyes upon, go back to stay with him in his castle forever.

BELLE: And I'm the first person you've seen?

MAURICE: I'm afraid so, but I don't want you to go-

BELLE: No, I must go, this beast spared your life. If in return for you to live I must go and live with a beast in a castle then, I must. A debt is a debt, you've always told me a man is only as good as his word.

MAURICE: Belle you mustn't go!

BELLE: And what if the beast were to come after you and come into the village and terrorise everyone who has done no wrong? I couldn't have innocent people put in harm's way because of me.

MAURICE: I couldn't be prouder to call you my daughter, you must go. *(BELLE goes to exit)* Belle, please look after yourself. I will love you forever.

BELLE: I will Father, I love you too. *(Exit BELLE)*

Song 6 – MAURICE

(Song ends. LUCAS enters followed by BEAUREGARD and MARCEL)

LUCAS: Ah! Maurice, why ze glum face monsieur?

MAURICE: Oh, Lucas it's you.

LUCAS: Yes, it's me. Wonderful is not it.

MAURICE: Belle is gone.

LUCAS: No worry, I am sure she will be back!

BEAUREGARD: Sir, what I think he means is-

LUCAS: Silence Beauregard! How long will Belle be?

MAURICE: An eternity

LUCAS: Good. How long is eternity, I av a very busy day.

MARCEL: Forever Sir.

LUCAS: Silence Marcel!

MAURICE: He's right, she's gone forever.

LUCAS: Forever, but how will I marry her now?

MAURICE: I don't think you'd be marrying her anyway!

BEAUREGARD: Sorry to but in but what's happened?

MAURICE: She has been taken captive by a Beast in a Castle in the Kingdom of *(local reference)*!

BEAUREGARD & MARCEL: A Beast?! *(MARCEL jumps into BEAUREGARD'S arms)*

LUCAS: *(local reference)*?! That is almost as bad as *(local reference)*!

MAURICE: It's true, she's being held captive at the Beast's castle and

it's all my fault.

LUCAS: So, what you're saying is you need a hero, who is butch, striking, and incredibly talented!

BEAUREGARD: *(Putting down MARCEL)* Where would we find someone like that?

LUCAS: I mean me! You buffoon!

BEAUREGARD: Oh yes of course Sir!

MAURICE: I don't know if I'll ever see my daughter again!

LUCAS: That is where I could be able to help you

MAURICE: What do you mean could be able to help me?

LUCAS: Well, defeating a beast takes a lot of courage and time.

MAURICE: Well what do you want in exchange for Belle's safe return?

LUCAS: Well now let me think… If I help you save Belle, I want your blessing for me to marry her!

MAURICE: What?!

LUCAS: You heard. I want Belle as my wife.

MAURICE: Never!

LUCAS: Very well, then you will never see her again! At least married to me she will be safe! What do you think boys and girls, should Belle marry me and be my ever-loving wife? *(audience: No!)* Oh shut up, I don't need ze opinion of peasants anyway!

MAURICE: Oh, I don't know! What do you think Marcel?

MARCEL: Well-

LUCAS: Silence Marcel!

MAURICE: I just don't know, you will look after her?

LUCAS: Of course.

MAURICE: And you'll slay the Beast and bring her back here safely?

LUCAS: Naturally, a beast will be no match for me!

MAURICE: No, I cannot do it. The man that Belle marries must be of her own choosing, only then can I give my blessing

LUCAS: You've made a very unwise decision Maurice, I don't need your permission to marry Belle if you're not around!

MAURICE: What? I don't understand?

LUCAS: I said, I don't need your permission and in fact I don't need you! Beauregard, Marcel!

BEAUREGARD & MARCEL: Yes Sir?

LUCAS: Take Maurice to the deepest depths of ze forest and leave him there for ze wolves!

BEAUREGARD: Pardon Sir?

LUCAS: You heard me, I can't av zis foolish old man get in ze way of me marrying his daughter, if he won't give me his blessing, zen he is of no use to me. Take him away!

MAURICE: You'll never get away with this!

LUCAS: Oh yes I will!

MAURICE: Oh no you won't!

LUCAS: Oh yes I will!

MAURICE: Oh no you won't!

LUCAS: Oh yes I will!

MAURICE: Oh no you won't!

LUCAS: Oh shut up! Be gone old man!

(BEAUREGARD & MARCEL are dragging MAURICE off together. Exit BEAUREGARD, MARCEL and MAURICE.)

LUCAS: *(Evil laughter)* So it's official Belle is to be my wife! And how can she disagree when I have her Father's blessing, after he so tragically died whilst losing his way in the forest, and besides do you really think once I've killed the Beast, that Belle will ever see anyone other than me again! Now if I am to defeat ze Beast I will need an army… I know those stupid villagers will follow me anywhere, besides I'd rather av zem get in ze way and die instead of myself, and once they've done ze most damage to ze Beast, I'll come in for ze final kill! *(Evil laughter)*. Don't you just love me?

(Blackout)

SCENE SIX

THE BEAST'S CASTLE

(The BEAST sits on a throne looking into his handheld magic mirror)

BEAST: My goodness! Marie, Pierre get in here now!

MARIE: What is it Master?

BEAST: The man that was here yesterday is repaying his debt and sending me his daughter!

PIERRE: How do you know?

BEAST: *(Showing MARIE and PIERRE, the Magic Mirror)* Look into my Magic Mirror, you can see anything you wish to see! Look you can see her on the way!

PIERRE: She could be the one to break the curse!

BEAST: Don't be so ridiculous, no one could love a beast like me

MARIE: Of course they could, underneath all of that fur is the lovely Prince I helped to raise from a baby!

BEAST: Why do you stay?

MARIE: I stay because I know there's good in you! I stay because I believe the curse can be broken!

PIERRE: Yeah, so maybe this woman being sent here forever is a good thing!

MARIE: All you have to do is be nice to her, show her the lovely man underneath all that fur. Maybe start sprucing yourself up a little-

PIERRE: Yeah maybe try some mouth wash and a shower!

BEAST: How dare you speak to me in this way!

MARIE: And maybe try to control your temper.

BEAST: WHAT TEMPER?!

MARIE: That one. Now I'll tell you what Sir, why don't you go off, get yourself cleaned up ready for her arrival. We'll make sure she's got a nice clean room to stay in.

BEAST: Very well *(Exit the BEAST)*

PIERRE: How is the girl coming to the castle going to fall in love with the Prince? I mean he's far more Beast than Prince these days!

MARIE: I know a thing or two about love. Love is about what's underneath-

PIERRE: What the floor?

MARIE: No! What's underneath-

PIERRE: Underneath your clothes? I don't know if anyone wants to see what's underneath your clothes!

MARIE: Oh you cheeky beggar! *(Clips PIERRE round the ear).* No, I mean your personality, beauty runs skin deep!

PIERRE: I think in your case beauty just ran and never returned.

MARIE: Oh, you rude boy! *(Clips PIERRE round the ear again)* I'll have you know many a man has fallen at my feet!

PIERRE: They must have got a shock when they looked up!

MARIE: The point I'm trying to make is this girl, who is coming to live in the castle, must fall in love with the Prince, regardless of his looks to break the spell.

PIERRE: How is she going to fall in love with him?

MARIE: Not a clue!

PIERRE: I think I can help!

MARIE: How's that?

PIERRE: We can use my new apple watch! *(Pulls out his apple watch, which is an apple attached to his wrist)*

MARIE: I must say I need to get one of those my blackberry is so outdated. Look, watch it doesn't even work *(she pushes a button the line 'Let it go' from Frozen plays).* See it's frozen!

PIERRE: *(Taps his apple watch and the line 'Into the unknown' plays from Frozen Two)* Oh no mines frozen too!

MARIE: Oh, I'm going to go and use the computer instead!

(All of the lines in quotation marks and block capitals are mimed to a track)

PIERRE: No wait 'DON'T LEAVE ME THIS WAY'

MARIE: Fine, let me see if I can help! *(MARIE goes to touch PIERRE'S apple watch)*

PIERRE: *(Moves out of the way)* Hey what are you doing 'YOU CAN'T TOUCH THIS'

MARIE: Fine. Is there anything that watch can help us with?

PIERRE: Hold on let me try the help button *(Presses the watch)* 'HELP I NEED SOMEBODY'

MARIE: Well that didn't seem to help at all! Do you have any food ordering apps on there? At least we could prepare dinner a bit easier!

PIERRE: Yeah hang on do you want; 'MCDONALDS, MCDONALDS, KENTUCKY FRIED CHICKEN AND A PIZZA HUT'

MARIE: Just a McDonald's will do

PIERRE: 'I'M LOVIN' IT'

MARIE: Hang on what about cleaning products? You'll have to order some more online-

PIERRE: Oh yeah, we're completely out of 'FLASH'

MARIE: What about ringing that Jean Val Jean to help us out with a few bits, what was his number again?

PIERRE: '24601'

MARIE: No, actually scrap that last time he was here, he built a huge barricade.

PIERRE: Yeah, but at least he was honest and told us 'I BROKE A WINDOW PAYNE'

MARIE: True, I suppose when that girl arrives, we'll have to have a party with dancing

PIERRE: 'BUT I DON'T FEEL LIKE DANCING'

MARIE: Yes, you never were much of a mover.

PIERRE: What?! I've got great moves, I was always good at the 'Y.M.C.A' and I could always do a brilliant 'AGADOO' and I was always the first to say 'COME ON, SHAKE YOUR BODY BABY, DO THE CONGA'

MARIE: But-

PIERRE: 'DON'T STOP ME NOW'

MARIE: Look back to it, what can we serve for dessert this evening?

PIERRE: 'I'VE GOT A LOVELY BUNCH OF COCONUTS'

MARIE: Coconuts for dessert?

PIERRE: 'MOCHA CHOCOLATA, YA YA'

MARIE: That's more of a beverage than a dessert. Is there anything else to do?

PIERRE: 'NO, NO, NO, NO, NO, NO, NO, NO, NO, NO, NO, NO, NO, NO'

MARIE: So, I guess that's everything sorted then!

PIERRE: Well, I'm glad that's everything sorted! I've got somewhere to be!

MARIE: Oh, and where's that?

PIERRE: 'BARCALONA'

MARIE: We can't afford to go there!

PIERRE: Yeah, I know, 'WE'RE GOING DOWN TO MARGATE' instead

(The doorbell rings)

MARIE: Well we'll have to go another day! I think she's here!

PIERRE: 'SOMEONE KNOCKING AT THE DOOR'

MARIE: Stop playing around with that watch and go and see who's knocking at the door

PIERRE: I don't understand why she's knocking when you can 'YOU CAN RING MY BELL, RING MY BELL'

MARIE: She'll have to come back tomorrow at this rate!

PIERRE: But what 'IF TOMORROW NEVER COMES'

MARIE: Oh, never mind! *(Shouts)* The door is open please come in! Now come on Pierre we best go and make sure her room is ready!

(Exit MARIE)

PIERRE: 'TIME TO SAY GOODBYE'

(PIERRE is pulled off stage by a hook. Exit PIERRE. Comedy Play off.)

BELLE: Hello, is anyone here? Hello? *(Spots the enchanted rose on the side of the stage)* Oh, look at that, I wonder what that's doing there?! *(Goes toward the Enchanted Rose) (Audience: Marie!)*

MARIE: Who's going near the Enchanted Rose! Oh Hello! Welcome to the Castle!

BELLE: Hello, you must be the Beast?

MARIE: I beg your pardon?

BELLE: The Beast, you know, tall man, broad shoulders, deep voice-

MARIE: I'm not the Beast!

BELLE: Oh, my apologies!

MARIE: That's quite alright, I've been called worse!

BELLE: I was sent here, as the Beast spared my Father's life, and in return the first person he saw had to come here for an entirety.

MARIE: And you were the first person?

BELLE: I'm always the first person my Father sees when he comes back home.

MARIE: Oh, you poor dear, well I promise you it's not that bad here. Oh, I haven't even told you my name, I'm Madame Marie Macaroon, but you can of course just call me Marie.

BELLE: Very nice to meet you Marie, my name's Belle.

(Enter PIERRE)

PIERRE: Hiya Gang!

BELLE: Oh hello, who are you?

PIERRE: I'm Potty Pierre! But most people just call me, oi you get down from my window.

BELLE: Potty Pierre?

PIERRE: Oh yeah, it's because I wash the pots here!

MARIE: Just call him Pierre!

BELLE: Why?

MARIE: Because that's his name.

BELLE: So then, Marie and Pierre, where is this Beast?

MARIE: He's just getting ready.

PIERRE: Yeah, he's just fluffing his hair.

(We hear a roar from the BEAST offstage)

BELLE: He doesn't sound very friendly

PIERRE: No, he just had a bad curry last night

MARIE: I'll get him, I know he's very excited to meet you. *(Shouts)* Master! We have company!

(Enter the BEAST)

BEAST: *(Roars)* So you are the one that is here for eternity!

BELLE: Yes, I am, my name is Belle, what's yours?

BEAST: Wait do I not scare you?

BELLE: Why would you scare me, I don't even know you

BEAST: This will be your humble abode for the rest of eternity-

BELLE: Actually, I was going to ask about that, can my Father not come and live here as well?

BEAST: No! That was not part of the deal!

BELLE: But-

BEAST: No ifs or buts! You will join me for dinner this evening!

BELLE: Is that a request or a demand?

BEAST: Don't talk back to me!

MARIE: Sir remember what we said about your temper

BEAST: I DON'T HAVE A TEMPER! Now Marie, Pierre fix us dinner in the main dining room. Belle I will see you there at six o'clock this evening, it would be in your best interest to be there! *(Exit BEAST)*

BELLE: What a horrible fur-ball!

PIERRE: *(To MARIE)* So breaking the curse is off to a great start, first woman here in years, he's already shouted at her and forced her on a date with him.

MARIE: Shut up Pierre go and start dinner!

PIERRE: Very well! See you in a bit *(Exit PIERRE)*

MARIE: Come on Belle, I'll show you to your room. It's got a lovely
  sea view!

(Exit MARIE and BELLE. Enter FAIRY disguised as a maid)

FAIRY: Bonjour again, I'm back!
  The Beast needs a nudge, or this curse will never budge
  Incognito I will stay,
  I'm in disguise, to help break the curses ties
  As the rose petals fall,
  The Beast is good and true, it's love he needs to pursue
  Silently I'll watch keeping an eye,
  Only love can break the curse, then the spell will reverse
  Maybe I'll just check the Rose
  The petals are falling, as the end of the curse is calling

*(FAIRY moves toward the Enchanted Rose. (Audience: Marie!)
Enter MARIE)*

MARIE: Oi, you keep away from that rose! Hang on who are you?

FAIRY: I am a new Maid here at the castle!

MARIE: A new Maid? Why we've not had new staff here in years!

FAIRY: *(Waves her wand, which has been concealed on her person in
  front of MARIE'S face, casting a spell over her. MARIE goes
  into a trance like state)* I am a Maid here.

MARIE: *(In a trance)* You are a Maid here.

FAIRY: I've been here for years. My name's Antoinette.

MARIE: *(Still in a trance)* You've been here for years. Your name is
  Antoinette.

FAIRY: *(Waves her wand and MARIE snaps out of the trance and
  FAIRY puts her wand away once again)* Hello, Marie what
  would you like me to do?

MARIE: Antoinette, I'm so glad you're here, we've got dinner to
  make and we need all hands-on deck!

(Enter PIERRE)

PIERRE: Hiya Gang! Hang on a second who's that!

MARIE: *(Said in a trance)* This Antoinette she's a maid, she's been here for years!

PIERRE: Oh no she hasn't!

FAIRY: Oh yes she has!

PIERRE: Oh no she hasn't!

FAIRY: Oh yes she has!

PIERRE: Oh no she hasn't!

FAIRY: Oh yes she has!

PIERRE: Alright, fair enough maybe you have!

  (Enter the BEAST)

BEAST: *(To FAIRY)* Who are you?

MARIE: *(In a trance)* She's Antoinette, she's a maid, she's been here for years.

FAIRY: *(Gets out her wand and waves it once again, the BEAST, MARIE and PIERRE all go into a trance)* My name is Antoinette, I'm a maid here and I've been here for years.

BEAST, MARIE & PIERRE: Your name is Antoinette, you're a maid here and you've been here for years.

FAIRY: *(Waves her wand and conceals it on her person once again).*

BEAST: Antoinette, shouldn't you be helping Marie in the kitchen-

FAIRY: What do you think of the new member of the castle Sir?

BEAST: You mean Belle?

FAIRY: Yes, Belle.

BEAST: She's- She's- Well she's beautiful isn't she, but how can she love a hideous beast such as myself?

FAIRY: It's about what's on the inside that counts, you just have to let your personality flow and she'll see past your looks because that's how love works!

BEAST: Really?

MARIE: That's what we've been trying to tell you Sir!

BEAST: If someone was to fall in love with me, it would break this curse, and I could return to being the Prince I once was!

FAIRY: And you'd have fallen in love!

PIERRE: Sort of two birds one stone really!

BEAST: Please help me, I want Belle to see past this beastly face!

FAIRY: That's what we're here for!

Song 7 – BEAST, FAIRY, PIERRE, MARIE & CHORUS

(Song Ends with the BEAST sat at the table ready for dinner)

MARIE: Belle! Dinner is served!

(Blackout).

End of Act One

ACT TWO

SCENE ONE

THE VILLAGE SQUARE

Song 8 – LUCAS & CHORUS (This is performed as if LUCAS is rallying his troops)

LUCAS: Now listen 'ere everyone, we will storm ze beast's castle with a plan I like to call 'everyone get in front of me and go first'. Now some of you might die but this is a risk we must all take, apart from me as I must remain at the back!

MALE VILLAGER 1: Why do you need to stand at the back?

LUCAS: As I must bravely protect those at the back who are slower!

FEMALE VILLAGER 1: You're so brave!

LUCAS: I know! But you forgot I'm also handsome! Now you must all go back to your homes and get your pitchforks and anything you deem necessary to defeat the beast!

(Villagers all exit)

(Evil laugh) Those stupid villagers! Oh, don't you lot boo me! I'm ze most intelligent, beautiful, handsome man in the whole of France! Oh yes I am! *(audience: oh no you're not!)* Oh yes I am! *(audience: oh no you're not!)* *(Stamping his feet like a child having a tantrum)* I am! I am! I am! *(audience: You're not! You're not! You're not!)*. Oh shut up, I don't care about your opinion anyway! Once I defeat the beast, I'll marry Belle, and her Father and all of you lot will never see her again! Oh and I'll make sure she never reads another book ever again! *(Evil Laughter)*

(Enter BEAUREGARD)

BEAUREGARD: Sorry I'm late Sir, I got caught up getting this present delivered

LUCAS: A Present?

BEAUREGARD: Yes, I was on my way to the post office-

LUCAS: Oh, you don't want to send through ze post office!

BEAUREGARD: No?

LUCAS: No, you see because what they'll do is *(takes the gift from*

BEAUREGARD) they'll shake it about *(shakes the gift)* drop it on the floor *(throws the gift on the floor)* and zen they will kick it over zer! *(kicks the present across the stage as he is walking over to get the present)* Oh no, you don't want to send by the post office!

BEAUREGARD: No? Why not?

LUCAS: *(Handing the present back to LUCAS)* It might get broken!

BEAUREGARD: Oh *(goes to exit)*-

LUCAS: Where are you going now?

BEAUREGARD: To the train station Sir, I thought I might deliver the present via train instead

LUCAS: Oh, you don't want to send through ze train!

BEAUREGARD: No?

LUCAS: No, you see because what they'll do is *(takes the gift from Beauregard)* they'll shake it about *(shakes the gift)* drop it on the floor *(throws the gift on the floor)* and zen they will kick it over zer! *(kicks the present across the stage as he is walking over to get the present)* Oh no, you don't want to send by train!

BEAUREGARD: No? Why not?

LUCAS: *(Handing the present back to LUCAS)* It might get broken!

BEAUREGARD: Oh *(goes to exit)*-

LUCAS: Where are you going now?

BEAUREGARD: To the airport Sir, I thought I might deliver the present via plane instead!

LUCAS: Oh, you don't want to send through ze plane!

BEAUREGARD: No?

LUCAS: No, you see because what they'll do is *(takes the gift from BEAUREGARD)* they'll shake it about *(shakes the gift)* drop it on the floor *(throws the gift on the floor)* and zen they will kick it over zer! *(kicks the present across the stage as he is walking over to get the present)* Oh no, you don't want to send by plane!

BEAUREGARD: No? Why not?

LUCAS: *(Handing the present back to LUCAS)* It might get broken! Who is this present for anyway?

BEAUREGARD: It's for you, *(hands it to LUCAS)* Happy Birthday

(Exit Beauregard)

(Blackout)

SCENE TWO

THE BEAST'S CASTLE

(BELLE and the BEAST are having dinner)

BEAST: Are you enjoying your meal Belle?

BELLE: Yes, it's wonderful

(Awkward silence)

BEAST: So…

BELLE: Yes?

(BELLE and the BEAST freeze, as the FAIRY enters and waves her wand)

FAIRY: You see, this is why I'm here
The Beast has no charm offence, but I can help him make sense!
I'll cast a magic spell to help
The Beast is nervous no more, he is now steadfast and sure!

(Waves her wand)

Song 9 – FAIRY & PIERRE

(Song ends and we start as if the FAIRY'S song never happened. BELLE and the BEAST are sat back down at the table. Exit FAIRY.)

BEAST: If I could give you anything Belle, what would it be that would make you truly happy?

BELLE: I'd like to see my Father again

BEAST: Very well *(the BEAST takes out has magic mirror from his pocket)*, if you look into this magic mirror it will show you whatever you wish to see.

BELLE: *(Takes the magic mirror and gazes into it)* Oh no, it looks as though my Father is in trouble!

BEAST: Then you must go to him

BELLE: I promise as soon as I know my Father is safe, I'll come straight back!

BEAST: You needn't come back, I can't keep you here, you're not happy

BELLE: What makes you say that?

BEAST: Who would wish to stay with a Beast such as me?

BELLE: You know, when you're not shouting or roaring, you're actually quite pleasant.

BEAST: Thank you, it's been so long since someone showed true kindness to me. Why are you being so kind to me?

BELLE: Because I didn't know you, and beauty goes skin deep. I see past the fur and fluff to the man underneath.

BEAST: There used to be a man, but now there is only Beast.

BELLE: That's not true!

Song 10 – BELLE & THE BEAST

(Song ends. The BEAST and BELLE go to embrace, but they are interrupted)

(Enter MARIE & PIERRE)

MARIE: Did somebody say dessert!

PIERRE: Yeah, you did just now!

MARIE: Oh, be quiet Pierre!

BELLE: Go ahead Marie what have you got?

Song 11 – MARIE – Can Can Routine

MARIE: Well I got some cream cakes today,
Some crème brulee from yesterday!
Scones and Jam from overseas.
Some pastries from that bakery.
This ice cream here is rather nice
With a flake no don't think twice
This cheesecake left me in a daze
This apple tart I need to braise
Cream or Custard
Drizzle on your plate tonight Cream or Jam first
Smear it on your scone alright Just one Cornetto
Vanilla, mint or strawberry Rock from Clacton Lollipops or
doughnuts
In sugar or cinnamon
This is what is on the menu
Apple pie to name a few
French fancy that I have freshly made
Just wait til you try my fondue

It is made from chocolate
And perhaps Macaroon or two
Pumpkin pies with cinnamon
Our Bakewells we're not binning them
Trifles now with several fruits
My mini cups look so cute
And why not try a cherry pie
The carrot cake is worth a try
Fruit cake, sponge cake, any cake, I will bake
Until you're full
Come on now just try them all Taste my crumble
Apples, pears or bananas Rocky Road
Stuffed with extra marshmallow
Christmas Pudding
That's the one we set alight
Every year at Christmas time
Coconut cream with extra cream of course
Upside down cake covered in some pineapple
Chocolate mousses, topped with lovely strawberries
Custard cream cakes,I like the ones from M&S
Lemon square bars, citrus with some sugar in
Pomegranate mousse cake, or perhaps an orange cake
Battered Mars Bar, or an apple turnover
Coffee cake treat
Fruit sponge, Marzipan, Lime key, with tea or coffee.
This is what is on the menu Jelly with some ice cream
Or a healthy option would be watermelon
Come on now try my apple strudel
It's cooling by the window
You can have some too
My desserts are;
Delicious, decadent, and brave
I said my desserts are;
Enticing, with spicing, and icing, and cherries, and berries, and
creams, and dreams, and priming with timing, and looking
whilst cooking, and fixing whilst mixing, and whisking.
Please choose what you would like to eat.
Come please sit back and take your seat.
Try the baked goods, but watch the heat.
Dessert is now served.

PIERRE: Can you say that again?

MARIE: Not a chance!

BELLE: I'm actually alright for dessert. I have to leave to go and find my Father.

MARIE: You're leaving?

PIERRE: *(To the BEAST)* You're allowing her to leave?

BEAST: Belle's Father is in danger, I cannot allow her to be here when I know she is unhappy

MARIE: But what about the cur-

BEAST: It doesn't matter.

PIERRE: What's happened to your Father Belle?

BELLE: From what I have seen, I think he's lost in the forest.

MARIE: Well we can't allow you to go alone, me and Pierre will come with you!

PIERRE: Will we?

BEAST: Yes, go with Belle and ensure she remains safe

MARIE: We'll come back Master, I wouldn't want to leave you all by yourself.

BEAST: Then you must go! And I'll await your return.

(BELLE, MARIE and PIERRE exit.)

(Blackout)

SCENE THREE

THE FOREST

(MAURICE sits alone onstage his hands tied)

MAURICE: I think this might be the end. I do hope my daughter is safe, hang on what's that Rose doing over there!

(Goes towards the Enchanted Rose)

(Enter MARIE followed by PIERRE and BELLE)

MARIE: Hey, get your hands off my rose you!

PIERRE: Hiya Gang!

(BELLE rushes over to her FATHER)

BELLE: Father! *(Unties MAURICE)* What happened? How did you end up tied up alone in the forest?

MAURICE: It was that awful Lucas, he asked me to give my permission for your hand in marriage and when I said no, he left me here in the forest for the wolves!

BELLE: Oh, that horrible man, I knew he was no good!

MAURICE: He's far worse than we ever imagined! But I must ask, who are your two friends?

BELLE: Oh, how rude of me, well these are two of the servants from the castle this is Pierre-

MARIE: And I'm Madame Marie Macaroon.

MAURICE: And what should I call you?

MARIE: Anything you want! Belle, you never told me how handsome your Father was!

MAURICE: And on top of leaving me here to be eaten by the wolves, Lucas is on his way with an angry mob to murder the Beast!

BELLE: Oh no!

MAURICE: What do you mean, oh no?

BELLE: I got to know the Beast, and underneath all of that fur, and the terrifying roars, he's actually a kind hearted and wonderful man.

MAURICE: Well in that case we must stop Lucas!

(We hear a wolfs howl)

PIERRE: What was that?

MAURICE: Oh no, I think it was the wolves!

PIERRE: *(Knees knocking)* I don't like it I'm scared!

MAURICE: Oh Marie hold me!

MARIE: Gladly! *(Grabs MAURICE and pulls him close into her bosom)*

PIERRE: What are we going to do?

MARIE: I know! *(Lets go of MAURICE)* I'll tell you what, why don't we sing a song to calm us down, and this lot out here will tell us if they see any wolves! Won't you boys and girls! *(Ad lib as needed)*

SONG 12 – MARIE, PIERRE, MAURICE & BELLE

(As they sing a WOLF enters the stage and waves around behind the cast onstage)

MARIE, PIERRE, MAURICE & BELLE: There was a what? *(Audience: a Wolf!)* A Wolf? Are you sure? *(Audience: Yes!)* Where did he go? *(Audience: That way)* Which way? This way? *(Audience: Yes!)* Well, we'll have to have a look then! *(MARIE, BELLE, MAURICE & PIERRE all sneak round together in a line and the WOLF joins the end of the line and scares MAURICE who runs off being chased by the WOLF)*

MARIE: Oh!! Where's Maurice gone? *(Audience: the Wolf got him!)* the Wolf got him?

MARIE, PIERRE & BELLE: Well, we'll have to sing it again then won't we! Whoops!

SONG 12a – MARIE, PIERRE & BELLE

(As they sing a WOLF enters the stage and waves around behind the cast onstage)

MARIE, PIERRE & BELLE: There was a what? *(Audience: a Wolf!)* A Wolf? Are you sure? *(Audience: Yes!)* Where did he go? *(Audience: That way)* Which way? This way? *(Audience: Yes!)* Well, we'll have to have a look then! *(MARIE, BELLE & PIERRE all sneak round together in a line and the WOLF joins the end of the line and scares BELLE who runs off being chased by the WOLF)*

MARIE: Oh!! Where's Belle gone? *(Audience: the Wolf got him!)* the Wolf got her?

MARIE & PIERRE: Well, we'll have to sing it again then won't we! Whoops!

SONG 12b – MARIE & PIERRE

(As they sing a WOLF enters the stage and waves around behind the cast onstage)

MARIE & PIERRE: There was a what? *(Audience: a Wolf!)* A Wolf? Are you sure? *(Audience: Yes!)* Where did he go? *(Audience: That way)* Which way? This way? *(Audience: Yes!)* Well, we'll have to have a look then! *(MARIE & PIERRE all sneak round together in a line and the WOLF joins the end of the line and scares PIERRE who runs off being chased by the WOLF)*

MARIE: Oh!! Where's Pierre gone? *(Audience: the Wolf got him!)* the Wolf got him?

MARIE: Well, I'll have to sing it again then won't I! Whoops!

SONG 12c – MARIE

(As they sing a WOLF enters the stage, stands next to MARIE and holds her hand. MARIE stops singing and looks at the WOLF, they look back and forth at each other three times, on the third look the WOLF screams and runs off)

MARIE: Charming!

(Blackout)

SCENE FOUR

THE OUTSKIRTS OF THE VILLAGE

(LUCAS, BEAUREGARD and MARCEL are onstage with an angry mob)

LUCAS: Hello everyone, did you miss me? I didn't miss you! Now listen 'ere you rabble. If we are to defeat the Beast then I'll need to train you like you've never trained before! Right, now fall in!

(Everyone physically falls over onto the floor)

LUCAS: What are you doing?

BEAUREGARD: You said to fall in!

LUCAS: I meant get into a line! Get up!

ALL: *(Mutters of 'I wish he'd been clearer' etc)*

LUCAS: Right, now zer's not enough swords for you all 'ere. So, we'll 'ave to practice by using mops! Marcel hand out ze mops!

(A stagehand pops out from stage left)

MARCEL: Oh, look a stagehand! *(the stagehand hands out a mop to MARCEL who hands it to the next person. LUCAS is at the other end of the line, all of the mops are passed down to him and piled in his arms)*

LUCAS: What are you all doing!? You need a mop each!

ALL: *(Mutters of 'I wish he'd been clearer' etc. Everyone takes their mops, apart from LUCAS who doesn't need one)*

LUCAS: About face!

BEAUREGARD: What about my face?

LUCAS: What about it?

BEAUREGARD: You said about face, so I'm wondering what is about my face?

LUCAS: Get back in line!

BEAUREGARD: *(Salutes)* Yes Sir!

LUCAS: Finally. Now from the right number! *(Everyone begins to dance to a rhumba beat)* No, no, no! What are you doing?

MARCEL: We thought you said do the rhumba!

LUCAS: Why would I want a rhumba!

> *(Rhumba music starts again; they all begin to dance apart from LUCAS)*

LUCAS: Stop!

BEAUREGARD: *(Singing)* …In the name of love!

LUCAS: Be quiet, now listen to me!

BEAUREGARD: *(Throws down his mop)* Oh I give up!

LUCAS: Come on pick that up!

BEAUREGARD: Okay *(Picks up MARCEL)*

LUCAS: Not that! That!

BEAUREGARD: Very well. *(He puts down MARCEL and picks up a villager instead)*

LUCAS: Not that, *(picks up the mop)* this!

BEAUREGARD: *(Puts the villager down)* Very well *(BEAUREGARD picks up LUCAS)*

LUCAS: No, not me! Put me down!

BEAUREGARD: Very well *(He drops LUCAS on the floor)*

ALL: *(Mutters of 'I wish he'd been clearer' etc)*

LUCAS: This is utterly useless, I mean what are you going to do if you get attacked by the Beast?

MARCEL: Run away!

LUCAS: But what if you can't run away?

BEAUREGARD: Then I'll run the other way!

LUCAS: Silence Beauregard! Now look 'ere none of you look fit enough to defend against ze Beast, so let's do some fitness! Now copy me!

ALL: Now copy me!

LUCAS: No, not yet!

ALL: No, not yet!

LUCAS: I said not yet!

ALL: I said not yet!

LUCAS: You're all beginning to annoy me!

ALL: You're all beginning to annoy me!

LUCAS: She sells, sea shells on ze seashore

ALL: She sells, sea shells on ze seashore

LUCAS: How can a clam cram in a clean cream can?

ALL: How can a clam cram in a clean cream can?

LUCAS: I'm not ze pheasant plucker, I'm ze pheasant plucker's son, And I'm only plucking pheasants till ze pheasant pluckers come

ALL: I'm not ze pheasant plucker, I'm ze pheasant plucker's son, And I'm only plucking pheasants till ze pheasant pluckers come

LUCAS: Look, just do what I do! *(He runs on the spot)*. One, two, one, two, one, two, as if you're riding a bicycle.

(All of them carry on running on the spot apart from BEAUREGARD who stops and leans on his mop)

LUCAS: What do you think you're doing?

BEAUREGARD: I'm freewheeling!

(They all burst into laughter apart from LUCAS)

LUCAS: Oh, I give up! Put ze mops away!

BEAUREGARD: No, I think we've got it! Forward March! *(BEAUREGARD and the villagers all perform a military routine to the tune of 'The Colonel Bogey March')*

(Exit Marching off BEAUREGARD, MARCEL and the villagers, leaving LUCAS onstage)

LUCAS: So, my little army seems to be ready! But they are mere cannon fodder, they will die at ze hands of ze Beast, giving me enough time to stroll in at the end, when ze Beast is completely exhausted, and kill him! But, quite possibly best of all, I'll marry Belle whether she likes it or not! Don't you just love me? *(Evil laughter)*

(Blackout)

SCENE FIVE

THE BEAST'S CASTLE

(The BEAST sits on his throne, MARIE, PIERRE, BELLE and MAURICE rush in)

PIERRE: Hiya Gang!

MARIE: Sir! We need to tell you something-

BEAST: Listen to me-

PIERRE: It's really important Sir

BEAST: Very well

PIERRE: *(Said with great pace)* Well you see Sir, it's like this; there's this horrible bloke called Lucas who wants to marry Belle, but Belle doesn't want to marry him, but he's quite pushy about it all saying he'll marry her anyway, but that Lucas man is coming here with a mob to kill you so he can marry Belle, he also threw Maurice, that's Belle's Father, who I believe you've already met, to the wolves in the forest, like I said not really a nice bloke, actually a bit of a nasty bloke, but anyway we found Maurice, Belle's Dad in the forest and he told us all about Lucas and his awful plans, then we got stalked by wolves, but we managed to escape, so we ran here really fast to tell you all about this in the hope that you'd know what to do, and I think that about brings us up to speed.

BEAST: Very well, Marie and Pierre barricade the front door! Belle, please go upstairs to safety-

BELLE: What? I'm not going upstairs I'm here to fight!

BEAST: But Belle I can't have you in harms way because I- because I-

BELLE: Because you what?

BEAST: I just can't have you in harms way! Now go upstairs and do as I say!

BELLE: *(Roared at the BEAST and everyone else, when she shouts it makes everyone almost fall backwards)* I SAID NOOOOOOOOOOOOOOOOO!

BEAST: *(Pause)* Very well, you can help.

BELLE: Thank you

MARIE: And I thought the Beast had roar on him!

BEAST: Now where is Antoinette?

(Enter FAIRY still disguised as Antoinette)

FAIRY: Here Sir!

BEAST: I need you to go with Maurice and stay on lookout from the tallest tower of the castle

FAIRY: Very good Sir

BEAST: Now everyone do as I ask!

(Everyone exits off apart from BELLE and the BEAST)

FAIRY: *(From offstage)* They're nearly here Sir, I can see them approaching the castle now!

MARIE: *(From offstage)* The door is barricaded!

BELLE: What now?

BEAST: We wait, but I don't think we'll be waiting very long!

BELLE: What was it you were going to say earlier on, when you were stuttering?

BEAST: Nothing.

BELLE: Because I love you too *(a loud crash is heard as several villagers burst into the castle, a fight ensues between the Villagers and the BEAST. During the middle of the fight BELLE shouts)* Stop! I said stop!

MALE VILLAGER 1: Belle, what are you doing here?

MALE VILLAGER 2: Surely you can't be friends with this Beast?

BELLE: This Beast means you no harm, you must look beyond the fur to realise underneath is a person.

(Enter MARIE and PIERRE)

MARIE: It's true, we've worked for him for years, and he's always been nice to us!

(Enter LUCAS followed by BEAUREGARD & MARCEL)

LUCAS: What is this? Why are you not killing the Beast?

VILLAGER 1: Belle says he's harmless-

LUCAS: Harmless? Look at him! He's a big ugly Beast!

(Enter MAURICE)

MAURICE: The only Beast here is you Lucas! When I said that you couldn't marry my daughter you had me carried away into the forest and left for the wolves!

VILLAGERS: *(Gasps etc)*

BEAUREGARD: It's true!

LUCAS: Beauregard silence!

MARCEL: But he's right!

LUCAS: Shut up Marcel!

BEAUREGARD: No, it's about time we stood up to you, you're nothing more than a bully and a coward!

MARCEL: Yeah! I agree with what he said!

LUCAS: Well, I don't need you two anyway, I will kill the Beast myself! *(Draws his sword)*. Engarde you filthy Beast!

BEAST: Very well *(The BEAST draws his sword. The BEAST and LUCAS fight, LUCAS eventually gets the better of the BEAST)*

LUCAS: No disgusting Beast is a match for me! Now Belle, will you marry me?

BELLE: Never! *(Takes the BEAST sword and draws it)*

LUCAS: Put ze sword down you silly girl! *(BELLE takes a swing at LUCAS, BELLE and LUCAS fight with BELLE getting the best of LUCAS, knocking away his sword and taking him down to his knees)*

ALL: *(Cheer etc.)*

LUCAS: No, please 'ave mercy I'm too pretty to die!

MARIE: Well, what do you think we should do with him girls and boys?

(Enter FAIRY)

FAIRY: I have a better idea! *(revealing her identity)*

PIERRE: She's a Fairy! I've always dreamed of meeting a Fairy!

MARIE: Careful son that's how I started!

FAIRY: I've been here watching this tale unfold
Belle you are so brave, Lucas must learn to behave!
I'll cast a spell to last forever and ever
Lucas, this is what's in store, you'll be good and kind forever more!
If this spell is ever broken Lucas
You'll spend your days as a frog, eating flies on a log!

(FAIRY waves her wand and LUCAS gets up from the ground)

LUCAS: Oh, what a lovely looking lot you are! Here have some sweeties! *(Throws some sweeties out into the audience)* I love you all so much! *(LUCAS skips off and exits)*

FAIRY: And Beast or should I say Prince Beaumont!
Belle loves you I can tell, she said it as the final petal fell!
Beast no more, arise as you once were!
The curse is broken and the true Prince inside is awoken!

(The FAIRY waves her wand and the beast is transformed into PRINCE BEAUMONT)

BEAST: *(Looking at his hands)* I never thought this day would come! Belle, you've saved me and there's only one thing I'd like to ask you. *(Goes down on one knee)* Belle, will you marry me?

BELLE: Oh yes of course I will!

(BEAST and BELLE embrace)

ALL: *(Cheer etc.)*

MAURICE: Marie, what do you say we make it a double whammy?

MARIE: You want to marry me?

MAURICE: Of course, you look so surprised!

MARIE: Not half as surprised as you're going to look on the first night of our honeymoon!

PIERRE: Well would you look at that a happy ending!

Song 13 – All

SCENE SIX

IN FRONT OF TABS/THE CASTLE

PIERRE: Hiya Gang! Have you all had a good time? *(Audience: Yeah!)* Good I'm glad you've all enjoyed yourselves. But do you know I've always wondered what I'd do if I didn't do pantomime…

Song (Routine) 14 – If I Were not in Pantomime – PIERRE, MARIE, BEAUREGARD, MARCEL, MAURICE, BELLE, BEAST and FAIRY

PIERRE: If I were not in Pantomime, something else I'd rather be
If I were not in Pantomime, a policeman I would be,
You'd hear me all day long singing out this song;
Evening all, hold it there, you can pass on through
Evening all, hold it there, you can pass on through

BEAUREGARD: If I were not in Pantomime, something else I'd rather be
If I were not in Pantomime, a milkman I would be,
You'd hear me all day long singing out this song;
Full fat cream, semi skimmed, put it on the step
Full fat cream, semi skimmed, put it on the step

MARIE: If I were not in Pantomime, something else I'd rather be
If I were not in Pantomime, an Interrogator me,
You'd hear me all day long singing out this song;
Confess young man, confess young man, Oh you naughty boy!
Confess young man, confess young man, Oh you naughty boy!

MARCEL: If I were not in Pantomime, something else I'd rather be
If I were not in Pantomime, a Nanny I would be,
You'd hear me all day long singing out this song;
Close your eyes, go to sleep, cutchy cutchy coo
Close your eyes, go to sleep, cutchy cutchy coo

MAURICE: If I were not in Pantomime, something else I'd rather be
If I were not in Pantomime, a Rugby Player me,
You'd hear me all day long singing out this song;
Score a try, kick a goal, back upon the spot
Score a try, kick a goal, back upon the spot

BEAST: If I were not in Pantomime, something else I'd rather be
If I were not in Pantomime, a Tennis Player me,
You'd hear me all day long singing out this song;

The ball was in, the ball was out, you can't be serious
The ball was in, the ball was out, you can't be serious

FAIRY: If I were not in Pantomime, something else I'd rather be
If I were not in Pantomime, a Traffic Warden me,
You'd hear me all day long singing out this song;
You can't park here, you can't park there, double yellow line
You can't park here, you can't park there, double yellow line

BELLE: If I were not in Pantomime, something else I'd rather be
If I were not in Pantomime, a Cleaner I would be,
You'd hear me all day long singing out this song;
Dusting here, dusting there, dusting cobwebs everywhere!
Dusting here, dusting there, dusting cobwebs everywhere!

ALL: Something else I'd rather…

BEAUREGARD & MARCEL: You could be home watching TV
Which is surely a smart place to be
I'm fully aware
You'd rather be there
But instead you're stuck here with me

ALL: Something else I'd rather…

MARIE: I saw a young man from Clacton
Boy I how really attract 'em
I give 'em kiss
Though they give it a miss
When they find out I'm butcher than them

ALL: Something else I'd rather…

PIERRE: Mum makes a banana cream split
With sugar and treats stuffed in it
But the cream had gone off
I started to cough
And now the toilets covered in- (All Cast Gasp) What?

ALL: Something else I'd rather…
Na Na Na Na Na Na Na Na
Na Na Na Na Na Na Na Na
Something else I'd rather…

*(All cast exit off during the Na, Na, Na's apart from PIERRE
who is left alone onstage)*

PIERRE: Be!

(Song Ends)

PIERRE: Well that was fun! Hang on a minute I might as well do it one last time! Hiya Gang! Hang on what's that Rose doing over there! *(Goes towards the Enchanted Rose. Enter MARIE)*

MARIE: Oi! Get away from that rose! Oh, Pierre it's you! Actually, I don't think Prince Beaumont will be needing this Enchanted Rose now that the curse is broken, and he's no longer a beast! *(Takes the Enchanted Rose and hands it off into the wing)*

PIERRE: Well how about that, everything worked out in the end. The curse is broken-

MARIE: I'm getting married!

PIERRE: And so are Belle and the Beast- I mean Belle and Prince Beaumont!

MARIE: I'm so happy I could sing a song!

PIERRE: Well that's handy because we know one!

MARIE: Do we? Well isn't that a stroke of luck!

PIERRE: Music please!

SONG 15 – PIERRE & MARIE – Jelly on a Plate (Song sheet)

JELLY ON THE PLATE
Jelly on the plate
Wibble wobble, wibble wobble
Jelly on the plate

PANCAKE IN A PAN
Pancake in a pan
Flip it over, flip it over
Pancake in a pan

NOODLES ON A FORK
Noodles on a fork
Twirly whirly, Twirly whirly
Noodles on a fork

MARIE: Oh, that was so good Pierre!

PIERRE: It was but I reckon everyone should join in!

MARIE: Right then everyone on your feet!

PIERRE: And just to make sure you're all joining in we've had the words written up nice and big so you can all see them! *(the song sheet descends from the top of the stage)*

MARIE: Right then altogether, nice and loud! Music please!

SONG 15a – PIERRE & MARIE – Jelly on a Plate (Song sheet)

MARIE: Now that was good! But I think this side were louder!

PIERRE: Well that's funny because I thought this side, my side were louder!

MARIE: Well I tell you what how about a bit of a competition, my side will go first and then yours afterwards

PIERRE: But who can we get to judge it?

(MAURICE enters)

MAURICE: I'll do it!

MARIE: What do you reckon everyone, should we let him do it? *(Audience: Yes!) (Ad lib as needed)*

PIERRE: Right okay then we have our judge, you go first!

MARIE: Very well, right, my side here we go!

SONG 15b – MARIE – Jelly on a Plate (Song sheet)

PIERRE: It was good, however my side let's do it even louder! *(Ad lib as needed)*

SONG 15c – PIERRE – Jelly on a Plate (Song sheet)

MARIE: So, who's the winner?

PIERRE: Yeah who's the winner?

MAURICE: I have come to my decision and the winner is… This side! *(Pick whichever side was the loudest) (MARIE and PIERRE ad lib to whatever the decision is)*

MARIE: Right well I've got a wedding to get ready for I'll see you later on! Bye for now! *(To MAURICE)* Come on you! *(MARIE and MAURICE exit)*

PIERRE: Well I guess that just leaves us then! I'll tell you what let's sing it all together one last time, but this time the loudest you've ever sung it!

SONG 15d – PIERRE – Jelly on a Plate (Song sheet)

PIERRE: See you at the wedding! Bye *(Exit PIERRE)*

SCENE SEVEN

BOWS

FAIRY: And so, our tale has come to a close

MAURICE: I have a wife, my own delicate rose

LUCAS: I'm really nice, I'm bad no more

BEAUREGARD: We're all happier now of that I'm sure

BELLE: The Prince and I will live happily ever after

MARCEL: I hope you didn't find this show a disaster

MARIE: Me and Maurice will do just fine

PIERRE: This is my only other line

BEAST: So, whether you've come from far or near

ALL: We hope to see you all next year!

SONG 16 – Finale – All – Celebration (Final Cast Bow)

(CURTAIN)

(END)

Also by Joe Meloy and available from Beercott Books

Will our dashing Prince save the day? Will Dame Maisy Marmalade and Muddles be more of a help than hindrance? Are the Dwarfs actually Dwarfs? And will the #Selfie obsessed Evil Queen be stopped? Join us in the Pantomime story of Snow White & the Seven Dwarfs!

Packed out with hilarious comedy routines and of course plenty of audience participation this Panto will have the whole family laughing and asking for more! OH YES IT WILL!

Jump into the rabbit hole and join Alice in Wonderland! How mad is the Mad Hatter? Will the White Rabbit ever be on time? Did anyone actually steal the Queen of Hearts jam tarts? Alice meets Duchess Dolly Dollop and Wally the White Rabbit, as they guide Alice through Wonderland and round up all of their friends to take on the Evil Queen of Hearts and save Wonderland!

About the author

I'm Joe Meloy ('...the excellent pantomime dame...' British Theatre Guide) and I'm an Actor, Pantomime Dame, Producer and Panto Enthusiast. I attended my first Pantomime when I was three and instantly fell in love with one of the most entertaining forms of theatre, in my humble opinion of course!

I have been performing in pantomime myself for a number of years having played Widow Twankey to an Ugly Sister, there have been one or two occasions where I haven't been in the dress, but I much prefer putting on my dresses, fake eyelashes and lip stick!

I performed my first professional Pantomime at twenty-three years old playing an Ugly Sister in an adult pantomime. I returned the next year to perform as Widow Twankey, from there I went on to play in family pantomimes as; Widow Twankey (twice more!) Dame Dolly Dollop, Nurse Nellie, King Arthur and as Maid Joan for the Hazlitt Theatre.